T0050858

SPACE SURVIVAL

KEEPING PEOPLE ALIVE IN SPACE

ALICIA Z. KLEPEIS

CONTENT CONSULTANT
SARAH RUIZ
Aerospace Engineer

CAPSTONE PRESS
a capstone imprint

Edge Books are published by Capstone Press,
1710 Roe Crest Drive, North Mankato, Minnesota 56003
www.capstonepub.com

Copyright © 2020 by Capstone Press, a Capstone imprint. All rights reserved. No part of this
publication may be reproduced in whole or in part, or stored in a retrieval system, or transmitted in
any form or by any means, electronic, mechanical, photocopying, recording, or otherwise, without
written permission of the publisher.

Library of Congress Cataloging-in-Publication Data
Names: Klepeis, Alicia, 1971– author.
Title: Space survival : keeping people alive in space / by Alicia Z. Klepeis.
Description: North Mankato, Minnesota : Capstone Press, [2019] | Series: Edge books.
Future space | Audience: Age 10. | Audience: Grades 4 to 6. |
 Includes bibliographical references and index.
Identifiers: LCCN 2019003345 (print) | LCCN 2019010897 (ebook) |
ISBN 9781543572735 (eBook PDF) | ISBN 9781543572650 (library binding) |
 ISBN 9781543575217 (pbk.)
Subjects: LCSH: Life support systems (Space environment)—Juvenile literature. |
Space environment—Juvenile literature. | Space medicine—Juvenile literature. |
Survival—Juvenile literature. | Space flight—Juvenile literature.
Classification: LCC TL1500 (ebook) | LCC TL1500 .K54 2019 (print) | DDC 629.45—dc23
LC record available at https://lccn.loc.gov/2019003345

Editorial Credits
Mandy Robbins, editor; Laura Mitchell., designer; Jo Miller, media researcher;
Katy LaVigne, production specialist

Image Credits
NASA, 9, 12, 15, 16, 19, 20, 23, 25, 27, 29; Newscom: UPI/NASA, 11; ZUMA Press/TASS, 7;
Shutterstock: Dotted Yeti, 5; Wikimedia: NASA/Expedition 46 crew member from the Cupola, Cover

Design Elements
Capstone; Shutterstock: Audrius Birbilas

All internet sites appearing in back matter were available and accurate when this book was sent to
press.

TABLE OF CONTENTS

CHAPTER ONE

STAYING HEALTHY IN A DEADLY PLACE

Imagine being part of an astronaut crew in the middle of a mission to Mars. You will be gone from Earth for at least three years. You and your fellow crewmates must stay healthy to do your research. Your camper-sized spacecraft is all that protects you from the harsh environment of space. Your day begins with exercise. One astronaut rides a stationary bike. You go for a run on a treadmill.

Various activities help keep astronauts mentally healthy. You check on the vegetables you are growing. They remind you of Earth. Another astronaut uses **virtual reality** to have adventures in a world outside the spacecraft. It provides an escape from the cramped quarters your team calls home.

Mars is about 140 million miles (225 million kilometers) from Earth.

Space is a very dangerous environment for humans. But researchers are trying to keep astronauts safe and healthy as they travel ever farther away from Earth.

SPACE FACT:

Russian **cosmonaut** Gennady Padalka has spent 879 days in space. That's more than any other human!

cosmonaut—a Russian astronaut

virtual reality—a three-dimensional world created by a computer user where things on screen seem to come to life

FROM ANIMALS TO HUMANS

Before the first humans traveled into space, scientists researched ways to keep them safe once they left Earth. They sent dogs, monkeys, cats, and chimpanzees into **orbit** before people ever went. They wanted to find out whether living creatures could survive. If so, they wanted to know what effects being in space would have on their bodies. Scientists learned a lot from these animals, but, sadly, many of them died during their missions.

SPACE FACT:

Dogs named Belka and Strelka were the first animals to orbit Earth and come back alive. The Soviet Union launched them in August 1960.

Belka (left) and Strelka (right) were stray dogs before they became the first creatures to survive space flight.

Today scientists at the National Aeronautics and Space Administration's (NASA) Human Research Program (HRP) look at the many challenges people face while in space. Without technologies such as special suits and cabin air systems, even breathing wouldn't be possible in space. From designing comfortable housing to preparing nutritious foods, experts work hard to make sure astronauts stay healthy.

orbit—to travel around an object in space; an orbit is also the path an object follows while circling an object in space

SPACESUITS:
IMPROVEMENTS OVER TIME

One measure that protects astronauts is spacesuit technology. Spacesuits protect astronauts from the **vacuum** of space. Without spacesuits, astronauts wouldn't live more than two minutes. There's no air for humans to breathe there, so they couldn't get oxygen.

Spacesuits also allow people to survive the extreme temperatures in space. Without the protective atmosphere of Earth, temperatures can vary wildly. For example, temperatures on the moon range between minus 280 and 260 degrees Fahrenheit (minus 173 and 127 degrees Celsius).

Spacesuits contain a layer of a super-strong material called Kevlar. It protects astronauts from micrometeorites. These rock particles rain down in space and could rip through weaker material.

SPACE FACT:

It takes 45 minutes for an astronaut to put on a spacesuit. This includes time to put on special undergarments that keep astronauts cool.

Spacesuits have improved a lot over the years. They've become more protective and easier to move in due to high-tech, flexible materials. In March 1965, Russian cosmonaut Alexei Leonov went on the first space walk in a spacesuit. After just 10 minutes he had to come back inside, as the temperature inside his suit was dangerously high. Today's spacesuits allow astronauts to be outside the spacecraft for more than eight hours. Scientists are working on a spacesuit that could keep an astronaut alive for six days for future missions.

vacuum—space that is completely empty of all matter, including air and other gases

CHAPTER TWO

THREATS TO HUMAN HEALTH IN SPACE

The human body is suited to life on Earth. There are many threats to human health in space. One of the biggest dangers for astronauts is space **radiation**. People are exposed to radiation every day by sunlight. But Earth's **atmosphere** and its **magnetic field** help protect people.

Radiation is much more damaging in deep space than it is beneath the protection of Earth's atmosphere. It can increase the risk of cancer. It can also damage the central nervous system. This damage might cause changes in behavior. For example, people might feel more anxious or have memory problems. Space radiation could also affect a person's ability to think and reason normally.

SPACE FACT:

The ISS faces 10 times more radiation than Earth. But because it lies inside Earth's magnetic field, astronauts are protected from the radiation of deep space.

SOLAR RADIATION

Earth's magnetic field deflects solar radiation.

MAGNETIC FIELD

Space radiation can cause other problems too. They range from feeling tired and queasy to having heart disease or vision problems. Researchers are trying to find strong yet lightweight materials that could shield astronauts from the negative effects of space radiation. This will be especially important as astronauts go farther into space. There they will be exposed to space radiation for much longer periods of time.

atmosphere—the blanket of gases that surrounds a planet

magnetic field—the region around a magnetic body within which magnetic forces can be detected

radiation—dangerous energy emitted as rays, electromagnetic waves, or particles

Japanese astronaut Koichi Wakata floats freely in the ISS.

SPACE FACT:

Mars has 38 percent of the gravity of Earth, while the moon has 17 percent. This could mean astronauts have an easier time keeping their balance on Mars than on the moon.

GRAVITY

People on Earth stay on the ground because of an invisible force called gravity. This force pulls you toward the center of the Earth.

But gravity isn't the same in space. It gets weaker with distance. The gravity on the moon is about 17 percent of the gravity on Earth. Different gravity fields affect people's balance and their hand-eye coordination. When the level of gravity is a lot lower than it is on Earth, it is hard for people to tell which direction is up.

Gravity also affects a person's heart, bones, and muscles. Without gravity at work, a person's bones get weaker. An astronaut's bone density decreases by 1 percent each month without gravity. The ISS crew members exercise every day to help prevent bone loss and keep them fit for their return to Earth.

On a trip to Mars, astronauts will experience three different gravity fields. There is the "normal" gravity on Earth, **microgravity** on the spacecraft, and about one-third of Earth's gravity on Mars.

microgravity—very weak gravity

CHAPTER THREE

MENTAL TOUGHNESS IN SPACE

A long car ride with your family can feel crammed. Now imagine living in a small spacecraft with a handful of people for months at a time. You can't open the windows to get fresh air. Without new companions or the ability to get outside, you might feel sad. You might struggle not to fight with your crewmates.

One big challenge of space travel is **isolation**. Astronauts have only a very small group of people to spend time with. They may miss feeling connected to loved ones back on Earth. Luckily, there are ways to help counteract the effects of isolated settings. ISS crew members often video chat with family and friends on Earth. This helps them feel more connected despite their distance from home.

isolation—the condition of being alone

ISS and space shuttle crew members

LED Lights Help Astronauts Sleep

On Earth sunlight tells people it's time to be awake. But astronauts aboard the ISS see 16 sunsets and sunrises each day. This can throw off their sleep schedules. It's possible to adjust the different colors of light that LEDs put out. Less blue and violet light can help calm people and allow them to fall asleep more easily. Another setting on LED lighting could help make a spacecraft's interior feel more like daylight on Earth.

KEEPING SPIRITS UP

Astronauts have a great deal of work to do during their space missions. They conduct scientific research. They update computer equipment. They clean filters and check support systems. But they also must have fun and keep up their spirits. People are more productive in their work when they feel good.

Astronauts have many ways to both entertain themselves and stay healthy. Exercise helps keep them in good spirits and physically fit. Getting good sleep is also important to astronauts' mental health. Astronauts watch movies, read books, and play games.

Researchers are working on new ways to relieve stress and help crew members cope with the pressure of long space missions. One idea is using virtual reality to provide an escape from the cramped conditions. Astronauts could stroll through a virtual nature preserve or visit a virtual art gallery. They could even interact with avatars of their friends and family members. These options are being considered for future space travelers.

SPACE FACT:

Each astronaut might have only 883 cubic feet (25 cubic meters) of living space on a trip to Mars.

CHAPTER FOUR

TESTING AND TRAINING

Many problems can occur when traveling to space. Before any spacecraft goes into orbit, NASA builds models of its different systems and structures. Every system on a model is tested and must work perfectly. A test vehicle might be dropped into water, crashed on purpose, or even heated to 3,000°F (1,649°C) to mimic the extreme conditions in space.

Astronauts also train for various activities before going on a mission. Astronauts practice space walks by wearing spacesuits underwater. Conditions there are similar to the weightlessness in space. A massive swimming pool called the Neutral Buoyancy Lab contains mock-ups of different parts of the ISS. The astronauts can practice space walks there just like they do in actual space.

Astronauts Steve Swanson and Scott Tingle train for a space walk in the Neutral Buoyancy Lab.

In 2009, Desert Research and Technology Studies (RATS) team members ran an analog mission at Black Point Lava Flow in Arizona.

SPACE FACT:

The RATS team tests technology for space missions in the Arizona desert. Conditions there maybe similar to what's found on a dusty, dry planet.

ANALOG MISSIONS

Analog missions are a great way to help astronauts prepare for space missions. These field tests help scientists solve problems. Astronauts might test out new vehicles, robotic equipment, or communications devices for a future mission.

Analog missions sometimes take place in locations similar to the extreme environments in space. Before some of the first missions to the moon in the late 1960s and 1970s, astronauts went to Hawaii. The volcanic landscape there was like the moon. The astronauts scooped up soil samples using special hand tools designed for their moon expedition. They also practiced using the lunar roving vehicle that they would drive on the moon.

Today's analog missions help astronauts prepare to go to Mars or an asteroid. One recent analog mission took place in Russia. Six men stayed in a chamber the size of a small apartment for 520 days. Scientists studied how their behavior changed when living in cramped quarters. On this mission, some crew members felt depressed and exhausted. Some astronauts argued with each other and with mission control. Researchers who saw astronauts' problems on this long analog mission hope to fix them before a Mars mission.

CHAPTER FIVE

RESEARCH AND MEDICINE IN SPACE

Before astronauts travel to distant locations such as Mars, scientists must know how space flight affects their bodies. The ISS provides an opportunity to study human health in a microgravity environment. Researchers look at how being in space can affect peoples' immune systems. Crew members take samples of their own saliva, blood, and urine while in space. Researchers then collect these samples. They compare them to samples of these fluids taken before and after the astronauts' space flight. These samples can show any changes in peoples' immune systems during their time in space.

SPACE FACT:

By growing bacteria in space labs, researchers have made progress in finding a possible treatment for food poisoning.

Japanese astronaut Aki Hoshide finishes collecting his blood samples.

NASA Twins Study

Scott and Mark Kelly are identical twins. They were also NASA astronauts. In 2015 and 2016, Scott spent 340 days at the ISS. Mark stayed on Earth. As identical twins, Mark and Scott have very little difference between their **genes**. Because of that, researchers hope to learn if some of the health effects in space are a result of genes.

gene—a unit of heredity passed from parent to offspring which determines characteristics of the offspring

SPACE MEDICINE

Astronauts must be very healthy and fit. But they still suffer health problems in space. Astronauts can have vision problems because of how fluid builds up in their bodies while in space. If astronauts don't exercise, their muscles can shrivel and their bones weaken. Medicine can help with some space-related health problems. For example, certain drugs may be able to help slow bone loss in astronauts.

As missions get longer, space doctors will need to have the most advanced medical technology. Telemedicine is also going to be important. Health care professionals can use this technology to care for and treat patients who are in a different location. For example, a spacecraft's chief medical officer could send a picture of a crew member's rash to medical experts on Earth. Then the officer could get advice about possible treatments.

SPACE FACT:

In the future, robots might help perform surgery in space, just as they do on Earth. They can work even more steadily than a human doctor's hands.

ISS Expedition Commander Leroy Chiao checks the eye health of Flight Engineer Salizhan Sharipov.

CHAPTER SIX

STAYING ALIVE FAR FROM HOME

Eating in outer space is a unique challenge. To stay healthy, astronauts must eat food full of vitamins and minerals. But there are no fresh fruits or vegetables in space. The foods astronauts currently eat are freeze-dried and packaged months or years before. Keeping food from losing its nutrients for that long is challenging. Experts are experimenting with new ways of processing space food that use less heat or are faster. This may help keep astronauts' food fresh longer.

enough food to keep astronauts alive. But
in space would be a nice supplement
od. Gardening would also be a good activity to
ss. Getting to smell, touch, and taste fresh pro
stimulate the senses. Russi
fully grown

Astronauts Yuri Malenchenko (left) and Ed Lu (right) sit down for a meal of prepackaged food. Hot sauce and barbecue sauce float nearby.

Around 200 different beverages and foods are on the main menu at the ISS. They range from tortillas to scrambled eggs to chicken teriyaki. But astronauts still get bored with what they eat in space. They have also reported that their sense of taste is dulled. Researchers are working to make the foods tastier and more varied to keep astronauts interested in eating well. This is important because crews on long space missions will need to bring nearly all their food with them. They won't have the option to resupply.

A LONG WAY FROM HOME

On deep-space missions, communication lags
will make talking to people on Earth in real time
impossible. If there was an emergency near Mars,
it could take 20 minutes for a message requesting help
to reach Earth. Crews would wait another 20 minutes to
hear back from mission control.

Astronauts on a Mars mission would have to be
able to deal with any injury, illness, or equipment
failure on their own. They'd have to use whatever tools
or supplies were on their spacecraft. Researchers
on Earth are already looking at ways to deal with a
variety of medical problems in space. For example,
researchers at Stanford University are testing new
methods to treat heart attacks in space. Companies
are developing tools to diagnose and treat kidney
stones too.

Engineers, scientists, and doctors will continue
facing new challenges as humans try to travel farther
away from Earth. Their discoveries will help find
better ways to keep space travelers safe and healthy
throughout future voyages.

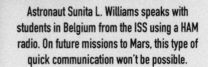

Astronaut Sunita L. Williams speaks with students in Belgium from the ISS using a HAM radio. On future missions to Mars, this type of quick communication won't be possible.

GLOSSARY

atmosphere (AT-muh-sfeer)—the blanket of gases which surrounds Earth or another planet

avatar (AV-uh-tahr)—a figure which represents a particular person, as in video games

cosmonaut (KAWZ-muh-not)—a Russian astronaut

gene (JEEN)—a unit of heredity passed from parent to offspring which determines characteristics of the offspring

immune system (IH-myoon SIS-tuhm)—the system of the body which protects it from foreign substances, tissues, or cells

isolation (eye-suh-LAY-shun)—the condition of being separated from other living things

magnetic field (MAG-neh-tik FEELD)—the region around a magnetic body within which magnetic forces can be detected

microgravity (meye-kruh-GRAV-uh-tee)—very weak gravity

orbit (OR-buht)—to travel around an object in space; an orbit is also the path an object follows while circling an object in space

radiation (rayd-ee-AY-shun)—dangerous energy emitted as rays, electromagnetic waves, or particles

vacuum (VAK-yuum)—space that is completely empty of all matter, including air and other gases

virtual reality (VUR-choo-uhl ree-AL-uh-tee)—a three-dimensional world created by a computer user where things on screen seem to come to life

READ MORE

Jefferis, David. *The Astronauts: Space Survival.* Moon Flight Atlas. New York: Crabtree Publishing Company, 2019.

Kluger, Jeffrey. *Disaster Strikes!: The Most Dangerous Space Missions of All Time.* New York: Philomel Books, 2019.

Mara, Wil. *Breakthroughs in Space Travel.* Space Exploration. Minneapolis: Lerner Publications, 2019.

INTERNET SITES

Five Hazards of Human Spaceflight Videos
www.nasa.gov/hrp/hazards-of-human-spaceflight-videos

Living in Space
www.esa.int/esaKIDSen/Livinginspace.html

Stay Safe in Space
airandspace.si.edu/stories/editorial/"taternauts"-and-spacesuits-how-astronauts-stay-safe-space

INDEX